I0606250

ICE AGE ANIMALS
STEPPE
BISON
BY ELIZABETH NEUENFELDT
ILLUSTRATIONS BY MAT EDWARDS
EPIC
EPIC, AN IMPRINT OF BELLWETHER MEDIA BY FLUTTERBEE

This edition first published in 2026 by Bellwether Media, Inc.

For information regarding permission, write to Bellwether Media, Inc., Attention: Permissions Department, 3500 American Blvd W, Suite 150, Bloomington, MN 55431.

Library of Congress Cataloging-in-Publication Data is available at www.loc.gov or upon request from the publisher.

ISBN: 9798893048186 (hardcover)
ISBN: 9798893049183 (ebook)

Editor: Betsy Rathburn Designer: Jeffrey Kollock

Printed in the United States of America, North Mankato, MN.

TABLE OF CONTENTS

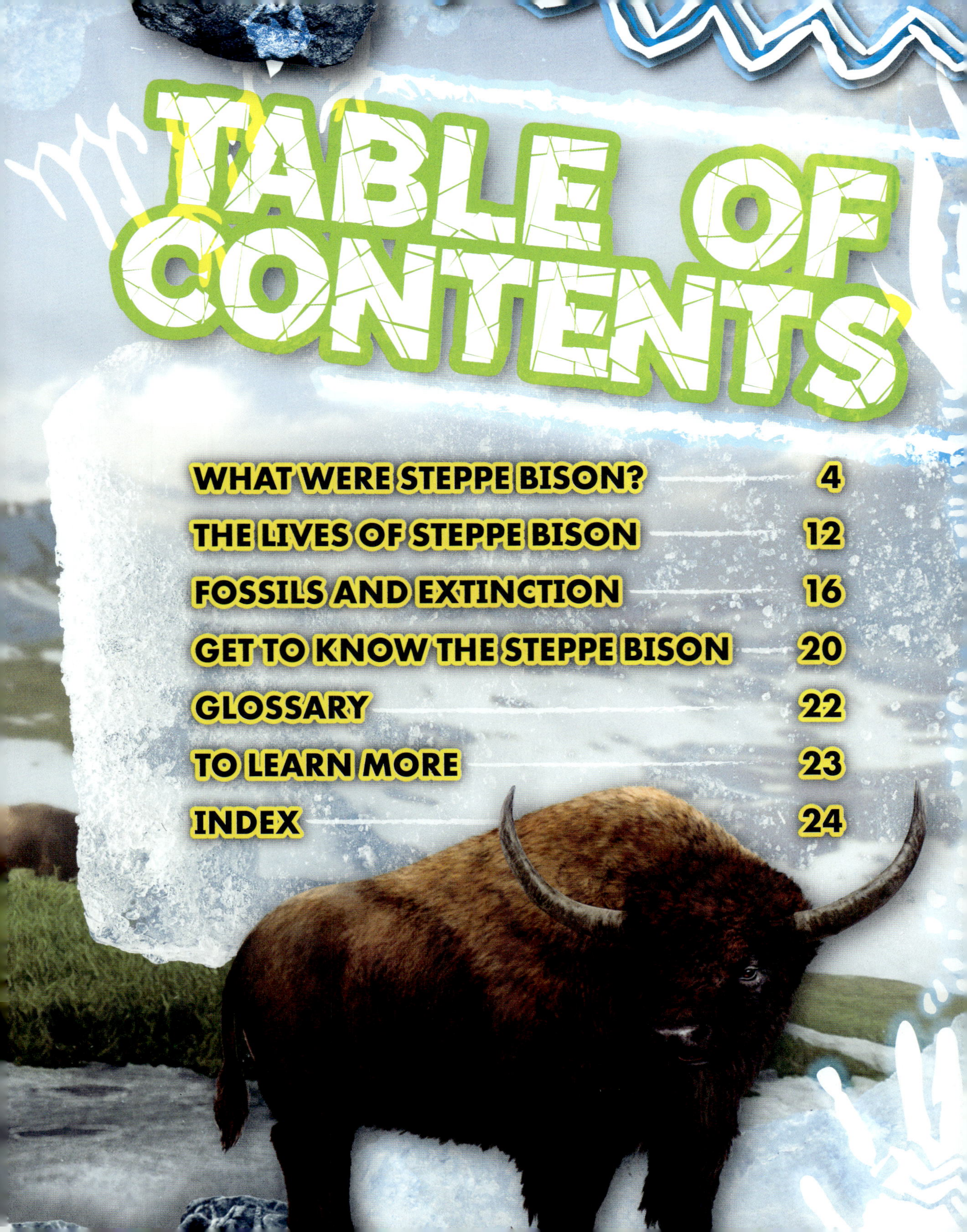

WHAT WERE STEPPE BISON?

Steppe bison were a kind of bison. They lived during the **Pleistocene epoch**.

They first lived in Europe and Asia. Then they spread into North America. They crossed the **Bering Land Bridge**.

These bison were big. They were over 6 feet (2 meters) tall at the shoulders.

They were around 9 feet (3 meters) long. They had strong back legs.

They had long horns on their heads. Their horns were about 3 feet (1 meter) long from tip to tip.

Males had bigger horns.
Female horns were smaller.

These bison lived in cold places. Their **manes** kept them warm.

Their backs had humps. These likely helped them clear snow. Finding food was easier.

hump
mane

THE LIVES OF STEPPE BISON

These bison lived on **grasslands**. They likely lived in **herds**.

They were **herbivores**. They ate a lot of grasses. They also ate shrubs and trees.

Early humans hunted these bison. They used bison for food. They made tools from their horns.

charging

Lions and wolves hunted them too. The bison fought back. They fought with their horns. They **charged** at **predators**.

CAVE DRAWINGS

Early humans drew in caves. They often drew steppe bison!

FOSSILS AND EXTINCTION

Most steppe bison died out around 10,000 years ago. They likely died from changes in **climate**. Early humans may have overhunted them.

PRESERVED STEPPE BISON

NICKNAME
Blue Babe

DATE FOUND
1979

WHERE
near Fairbanks, Alaska

Many steppe bison **fossils** have been found. Some are **preserved**!

BEHIND THE NAME

Blue Babe is named after Babe the Blue Ox. This is a giant blue ox. It is from stories about a character named Paul Bunyan.

Two kinds of bison live today.
They have humps. They have brown fur.
STEPPE BISON
hump
larger horns
brown fur
larger body

Bison today are smaller. They have smaller horns. Steppe bison are gone. Other bison live on!
EUROPEAN BISON
hump
smaller horns
brown fur
smaller body

GET TO KNOW THE STEPPE BISON
WHO FIRST DESCRIBED A PRESERVED FOSSIL?
Walter and Ruth Roman and their sons in
1979
DIET
grasses
shrubs
trees
brown fur
large body
WHERE DID THEY LIVE?
Europe, Asia, and North America

WHEN DID THEY LIVE?
around 1.2 million years ago
Steppe bison first appear
160,000 to 90,000 years ago
Early modern humans first appear
around 10,000 years ago
Steppe bison die out
hump
large horns
WEIGHT
=
around 1,543 to 1,764 pounds (700 to 800 kilograms)
HEIGHT
more than 6 feet (2 meters) at the shoulders

GLOSSARY

Bering Land Bridge—a large region between North America and Asia that has been partly or wholly above ocean waters in the past

charged—rushed to attack

climate—the usual weather conditions in a place

fossils—remains of living things that lived long ago

grasslands—lands covered with grasses and other soft plants with few bushes or trees

herbivores—animals that only eat plants

herds—groups of animals that live and travel together

manes—shaggy hair around the necks and heads of some animals

Pleistocene epoch—a time in history that lasted from 2.58 million years ago to 11,000 years ago and included the last ice age

predators—animals that hunt other animals for food

preserved—kept safe from being damaged or destroyed

steppe—related to dry, flat lands in areas with wide temperature ranges

TO LEARN MORE

AT THE LIBRARY

Bodden, Valerie. *Bison*. Mankato, Minn.: The Creative Company, 2023.

Gish, Ashley. *Ancient Bison*. Mankato, Minn.: The Creative Company, 2023.

King, SJ. *The Secret Explorers and the Ice Age Adventure*. New York, N.Y.: DK Publishing, 2022.

ON THE WEB

FACTSURFER

Factsurfer.com gives you a safe, fun way to find more information.

1. Go to www.factsurfer.com.
2. Enter "steppe bison" into the search box and click 🔍.
3. Select your book cover to see a list of related content.

INDEX

The images in this book are reproduced through the courtesy of: Mat Edwards, front cover, pp. 1, 4-5, 6-7, 8-9, 10-11, 12-13, 14-15, 16-17, 18-19, 20-21; Bernt Rostad/ Wikimedia Commons, p. 17.